Larry
Speare

MEMOIRS AND MEMORIES

DEDICATION

'To all the Marines killed in action in Malaya".

CONTENTS

ACKNOWLEDGMENTS

'Heartfelt thanks to Linda Perry for typing my words for this book and all those who have kindly contributed to editing and making it happen.'

1 INTRODUCTION

When it comes to telling a life story, it can be hard to decide where to start and what to include. What is a special memory to one person, may not be to another. What I may consider a trivial detail and not think to include, someone later can be left asking questions such as why, how, and when?

I started this process by writing notes, scribbles of stories and names, in no pattern or order just as they came to mind. Then I hit moments of frustration as I struggled with dates, not sure if I had them correct, and with places forgotten and misplaced in the memory of over 90 years.

I, however, still felt it worthy to start, to share my story, as I think I have had a rather interesting life and whilst lots of those close to me may have heard these stories before, I'd like to record a snapshot of these memories to be remembered, for my family and those who knew me. I'd also like to think those special memories and moments will not somehow get lost or be forgotten through time.

So let me introduce myself. Lawrence Ivor Speare. Known mainly as Larry now, I will tell you more about that later. I was born in Ford, Plymouth on June 5th, 1933, to Mother Ethel and Father Percival. Born with double Pneumonia, I had a difficult start in life. I was late to do almost everything. I didn't talk until I was nearly 7 years old.

My mother was my greatest supporter, she always encouraged me to better myself and be happy. My mother was born in Eggbuckland into a farming family and my dad was from a naval family, his father was a Naval Officer. When they married, they moved to a house in Bedford Street, Ford.

Photo: BACK ROW FROM LEFT: Friend from France, Ralph and Raymond
FRONT FROM LEFT: Sonny, Mum, Dad and Lorrie (Nickname I developed over the years)

I was one of six children, the second youngest. I had one sister, Edna and four brothers Maurice, (the oldest) Kenny, Raymond, and Ralph (the youngest).

2 FAMILY AND SCHOOL

Growing up as kids, we were very poor. The country was in recession, my parents provided as much as they could. We all went to school in Ford and later Crownhill Modern Secondary. My dad worked long days as a labourer, getting up at 4am to travel to the Royal William Yard, Plymouth to light fires in the Victualling Yard. He was paid £2.25 a week; my mother became a dress maker and clothes repairer when times got hard to help earn extra money to support us all.

Me and my brothers all got along well. We would get up to a bit of mischief pinching apples from local orchards and lighting bonfires whilst playing. The local constable had a daughter called Dorothy, who used to hang around with us boys and her elder brother Gordon Marks. Everyone used to say she liked 'Lorrie.' That was my nickname as a child, but in essence she was just a 'tomboy' who liked hanging out with us. Her brother used to tell us off, but we didn't get into any serious trouble. Apart from one time.

As boys in the 1940's we all smoked, and we got a packet of 'fags' and would all hide out in a local barn, socialising and messing around. We must have been between 11-14 years old at the time. One time we were at the barn and spotted a farmer marching up the path to the barn, probably to investigate the noise. We all ran away, and our friend Alfie Willis threw his cigarette down and it set fire to the hay. The whole barn went up in flames. Luckily enough no one was hurt but the police caught us. We were taken to court and got into a serious amount of trouble. Nearly all the boys left court crying, I was more scared of my mum than them, I hadn't cried in court and my mum would later recount how stubborn I could be by telling this story.

My mum was my greatest fan and supporter. If I ever got into trouble people would suggest it was because I was a little slow, or uneducated, but she would always stick up for me.

It was a lovely community where we lived and I can remember many friendly faces and people who were kind. Miss Brighton and her daughter Amanda, Margaret Park, then there was an Airman, a Sailor and a Merchant Seaman in our street but their names escape me.

During WW2, our home in Ford was bombed, meaning we had nowhere to live. We were given a small cottage with two bedrooms, a living room and kitchen, in Hartley by the city council of the time. It was a lovely community with many locals much better off than us. I remember a few of the kindest people, for example Mrs. Mundy, Admiral Munday's wife who used to bring my mother clothes and hand me downs for us kids. My mother was always humble and very appreciative of the support.

As a large family in a two-bed cottage, we had to make this work. I remember my mother and sister shared a room, myself and my brothers in the other one and my father would sleep on the landing. Our prize possession was a piano! My father was an amazing piano player and gave lessons, I can still see it now. It had two large candle sticks on top that we used to light in the evenings.

During the war, our lives changed, Maurice Percival Edwin Speare (The oldest of my brothers) worked for the Cooperative and as an Air raid warden during WW2 until he was conscripted at age 18 to join the Army. He was drafted to the artillery in France and was killed shortly before the war ended, crossing the river Rhine.

Photo: Me visiting Maurice's grave

Photo: Maurice in his Uniform a week before he was killed.

I remember the day we got told like it was yesterday. There was a knock at the door and I went to answer shouting at my mother who was cleaning the open fire out of dust. She said it was just the postman, so I ran to get the post and he presented me with a telegram. She asked me to read it to her and in that telegram was the news that Maurice had been killed. She cried like I'd never seen before, running next door to her friend Miss Ham.

Edna (My Sister) also worked as an air raid warden in WW2. She was engaged to a man for a long time, but our mum wouldn't let her get married till after the war and we as brothers hated the way he treated her and us. They eventually parted ways but not without trouble. He and his family took her to court for breach of promise, but he lost the case.

When the Americans arrived in Crownhill Plymouth, dances were set up and Edna met someone new. Leonard Mutter from Virginia who was a Sergeant in the infantry unit, nicknamed Sonny. They wanted to get married but again mum said no! But if he came back from war safely, then she would agree. We all respected my mum, and we did exactly what she wanted.

Kenny (the second oldest brother) was by far the most academic of the boys, he won a scholarship to go to Devonport High for Boys, he trained as an electrician and was conscripted to the RAF.

Raymond was also conscripted to the RAF. Raymond was probably the best looking of us brothers and always had the girl's attention. He was nicknamed 'angel face.' Which honestly, he did not really like. As younger siblings we would shout to him 'angel face' and run away quickly before he caught us. He was incredibly generous and kind. He would come home as often as he could to see us and bring us gifts. He was generous his whole life.

Ralph (The youngest of the brothers) joined the RAF at the age of fifteen as a boy apprentice.

Photo: FROM LEFT: Ralph, Lorrie, Raymond and Kenny

One day at school me and a few friends walked over to the fields that are now Whitleigh. There were no houses there at the time, but German prisoners of war were laying foundations and clearing the land. We had gone over to see if we could talk to them. The headteacher (Mr. Harris) found out and called us all in. He told the other boys they were not to speak with Germans as they were the ones who had been bombing our town. He dismissed them but made me stay. He said to me I don't like doing this, but you are getting the cane. It was just a few weeks ago you had the terrible news of what happened to your brother and now you are trying to talk to Germans. He said I should be ashamed of myself.

Crownhill Secondary Modern School was a good school. We used to go for morning prayers every day and then recite the school motto 'Manners maketh man.'

Photo: BACK ROW FROM LEFT: Mr. Cook, Miss Gander, unknown, Miss Howard
Mr. Hannaford FRONT FROM LEFT: Miss Olver, Mr. Harris, and Miss Trethewy
Photo Credit: Marlene Horton

3 ENTREPENEUR AND CONSCRIPTION

I enjoyed school but was always looking for something else. Near where we lived, Miss Ham (my mother's close friend) had a small shop called Vinstone Stores, in Hartley Vale. They used to offer deliveries via taxi, which was an expensive service and which most people did not have the money for. I had spotted this as an opportunity and so one day made myself a trolley. I cannot remember how or what out of exactly, I just knew I worked hard on that trolly. I went to speak with Miss Ham and offered to provide a delivery service with no set fee. She would offer her 'delivery boy' (me) to bring their shopping home and I would get paid around three pence to a shilling in tips. I always remember her saying 'you'll always find a way to make a few bob!'

I left school at fifteen and needed to find a proper job. I was chatting to my mother about what I could do and she said she had seen an advert for COOP, for a delivery boy for the laundry department. She took me to the local store where I met Manager Ted Delve, who asked me why I wanted a job, and I told him 'I had always wanted to work in a shop' and they gave me the job. Most boys my age were off getting apprenticeships in trades such as carpentry and building but I did not want a labouring job. I liked the buzz of the shop, the design and layout, the talking to people and the satisfaction of seeing someone get what they needed. Laundry boy was a hard labouring job however and not a position in the shop. I was collecting dirty laundry from hospitals and other places. The laundry was often dirty and heavy, and the COOP driver of the van would never help. My mum used to hate the dirty state of me when I came home, I hated the job!

Photo: Larry in Uniform

I was then conscripted. All boys at the time had to do at least 2 years service when they became eighteen. I remember being called to a local hall to stand in front of a board. To be honest they were very fair. They gave you the choice of which force to join RAF, Army, Navy or Marines and asked what you might be interested in or good at. My mother had given me strict instructions to choose the RAF as the only brother (Maurice) who had chosen otherwise had been killed and she blamed that on the Army choice. I, however, had always been fascinated with the Marines. A soldier on land and sea! I had read many stories that involved Marines and so I was set on this as my choice. I wanted to be a commando. I'm not sure if my mother had written them a secret letter or if it was because I was a nine stone slim teenager, but they questioned me lots asking me if I knew what the Marines did and asked if I would not prefer something else. I was sure. They made me wait in the corridor and when I went back in, they said 'Well Lawrence you have your wish.' I went home and my mother cried when I told her.

4 MARINES AND FIGHTING IN MALAYA

I joined the Marines in 1951 just before my 18th birthday and was first sent to Lympstone training camp in Exmouth, near Exeter. Here I did three to four months training before passing out. I was then told I was to be sent to Malaya with 45 Commando. I passed the physical test and was the proudest person in the land.

Picture of the Empire Pride troop ship

We joined the Empire Pride Troopship in Liverpool, travelling there by train, where it left for its long journey to Singapore.

Photo: Empire Pride deck – Larry second from right front, pushing out chest.

We travelled down through the Mediterranean to start with stopping for fuel and supplies. Anytime we stopped it was classed as leave so the whole time was spent with my colleagues who soon became friends. I remember being near Egypt and we had to take turns on deck two hours on and two hours off. Holding guns and waiting to be fired at as we went through the Suez Canal, until we came to the end near Aden. There was nothing but trouble in that part of the world at the time.

Photo: Larry in uniform in Aden

Dear Edna!

By the time you get this I'll be an my way to Malaya. I hope by the time I come back you will be over hear with Deanna & Sonny. I'll write and let you know how I'm doing. Give Braydene a big kiss from me.

All my love

Frankie

Photo: Letter Larry sent home to Edna

We stopped in North Africa for infantry training.

Photo: The desert

Photo: Infantry training

Photo: Larry and one of the other commandos taking a nap in the shade under a palm tree

We eventually ended up in Singapore where we disembarked and were put onto trains to travel up to North Malaya. Here we had a station camp where we would rest in between duties.

Photo: Larry and one of the other commandos on a camel

Our duties were long. In the heavy jungle, it was nothing like I can describe, it was both impressive and harsh all at the same time. Dense vegetation, tall trees, in some parts you couldn't see the sky, wild animals and heat and cold extremes like I'd never felt before. It was our job to patrol the area which was miles long.

Photos: The jungle Malaya

Photo: Larry second in from the left

Photo: Morning patrol meeting

We gathered every day to get our instructions, which would give us an idea of what we were walking into. If it was muddy, cold, hot and if they had recently been under attack. Traps and tricks. Before rolling out onto duty.

The Chinese Communist would hide out, intent on destroying rubber trees and various mines important to the British and Americans. They

thought if they kept causing trouble we would leave. It was our job to stop this. *Photo: Boats on the river in jungle.*

Photo: On patrol in jungle
Photo: Tanks leaving barracks

Photo: Cars on patrol with troops in jungle

Photo: Explosion in jungle

Photo: Rubber plant on fire

When the commandos pulled out, we were presented with the new colour by Prince Philip at Selarang Barracks in Singapore.

Photo: Invitation to event

Photos: The barracks in Selarang

Photo: The corridor of barracks in Selarang

We then travelled home stopping mainly in the Mediterranean to practice manoeuvres with the American Marines, spending some time in Malta and Tunisia.

Photo: The British with the American Marines on practice

Photo: Larry second from left

Photo: Larry at the back with the cigarette

We were all so close and got along, we were away from family and became each other's family. This was us on Christmas day. (Photo above)

Photo: All of us marching

Photo: Larry to the left with pal Rumsby

We managed to enjoy ourselves a little especially in Malta, me and the boys loved playing football.

Photo: Our Football team –Larry back right with my hands on my hips

Photo: Playing football

I was away for just over a year. In my discharge interview they tried to get me to stay but I had spoken to older Marines and their advice was " Janner (my nickname as I was from Plymouth) don't listen to what they promise you!" I had also been writing to a girl and missing family and I wanted to come home. So, I was discharged for completing all my agreed service time. Me and the lads didn't really keep in contact much, you must remember this was national service and lots of them hadn't chosen or enjoyed life in the Forces. Plus, back then it was more difficult to stay in touch with people from other parts of the country.

Photo: Enjoying the beach

Photo: Larry in uniform and medal

5 LIFE AFTER NATIONAL SERVICE

When the war was over, Kenny my brother was drafted to a special section of UK police Intelligence in Bristol. He was highly thought of in his job. He transferred to the police boat section in Plymouth. He married Shirley De-Mille but was taken ill suddenly at a young age and died of appendicitis in hospital. Shirley went back to Bristol, and we didn't see her again.

Raymond left the RAF and emigrated to the US where he worked for the American Army. He was transferred to Europe. He met Monique in France, where they married and had two sons. He then moved to Spain where he opened a garage. He was not a great businessman. He would rather give stuff away! He later moved back to England and divorced. He then married Carol and had two more children, Paul and Raylisha.

Ralph did 23 years' service in the RAF, before retiring. He never got married or had children.

Edna married her American soldier 'Sonny,' the love of her life at a ceremony in Eggbuckland Church. My mother made the wedding and bridesmaids dresses. They later moved to the US. They had four Children. Sonny went on to become part of the American secret service.

Photo: Sonny by crowd with black gloves on. On duty when the Queen Mother visited America

When I came home from national service the girl and I didn't work out and I was thinking about what I wanted to do. I returned to the new Cooperative on Royal Parade, in Plymouth to speak with the same Manager, Ted Delve. He told me he didn't need any more sales staff, but he would give me a chance with one condition. I had to go to night school to improve my education. He had worked with my brother Maurice for a time and had great respect for him, and as he was no longer around, I think he wanted to give me a chance. I went to night school at Western College, Mutley Plain and there I improved my level of education.

I became an apprentice and worked with man called Sam King in the Carpet department of the COOP on Royal Parade. I was only allowed to sell the rugs and doormats, as at this time only senior managers were allowed to offer fitted carpets. Fitted carpets were nearly always broad loomed and still quite unusual at this time and sold by the yard at around £1.11p per yard.

After a period of just a year, Ted Delve approached me and said how amazed he was at my sales and commitment to night school and said he wanted me to go and manage the Launceston Store. I was so taken aback, but accepted, I used to have to get the bus from Plymouth there and back every day. This too was a success, and I was then asked to manage a slightly larger store in Kingsbridge. In both cases now being able to sell the fitted carpets too!

I met my first wife Valerie. We were together about fifteen years and had two children, David and Amanda. I decided I wasn't too happy with what I was doing. We then decided to emigrate to Virginia, USA where my sister was living in 1954. Sonny (my brother-in-law) helped me get a job in the Army PX shop. It is here where my name was shortened to 'Larry' and has stuck ever since. We had a happy life, we travelled around America and really enjoyed ourselves. But we decided to move back to the UK as Valerie really was homesick.

6 SPEARE AND EDWARDS

When we returned to the UK. I started work for Phillips Furniture Store. I was a successful part of the sales team and Valerie and I were given a council flat in Whitleigh.

It was at Phillips furniture store that I met Charles Edwards. He was a wholesale rep that used to visit the store selling carpets and furnishings. He had been a guardsman during the war and was now a commercial traveler for a big national firm. We became friends, going out for coffee from time to time. One day he said to me 'boy I've seen how successful you are and have a proposal for you.' He always called me boy in our chats.

Photo: Charles on the left and Larry on the right at the Cornwall Street Store

He suggested we look to open our own store. I sold my only asset a Ford Anglia and Charles said he would 'bank roll' me for about a year and provided it was a success would then join the business as a partner and give up the travelling. This is when the company Speare and Edwards was born.

Photo: Larry working in Cornwall Street Store

We looked around and rented a small shop at 96 Cornwall Street, where we sold carpets trading as The Carpet Centre. The staff consisted of myself, Bob, who had just finished school, and Dennis, a carpet measurer and fitter. Charles and I made several contacts through his connections. I focused on advertising. Lots of shops were opening at the time and this store was a remarkable success.

Larry Speare

Photo: Evening Herald Newspaper announcement

Photo: Larry working in Cornwall Street Store

34

Photo: Speare and Edwards delivery van

So much so that we thought we could open another store, a bigger one, and so started looking for another lease for some new build units being built on Mayflower Street. When they had finished being built, in 1966, we signed a lease and opened another store which was bigger selling both carpets and beds.

Photo: Mayflower Street Store

We were getting noticed and reps from everywhere started visiting the store offering us deals and touting for business. Charles resigned from his job and joined the Cornwall Street store whilst I went to manage the new store in Mayflower Street.

Photo: Plymstock Store

Both these stores prospered over the years. We opened an old warehouse in the Plymouth Barbican and another large store on George Street. We then expanded even further by opening stores across Devon, in Newton Abbott and Exeter.

Photo:
Store

Photo:
Store

I became a little restless, as all these stores had leases so were rented, the rents were increasing more and more.

I suggested closing some stores, but Charles was not keen on this. 'Speare and Edwards' stores were doing very well, and we had opened even more stores in Plymstock, Paignton and Torquay. Seventeen in total!

There came a moment when we both wanted different

things in life and so we decided to split the partnership and go our separate ways.

Photo: Plymstock Store

7 A NEW CHAPTER IN BUSINESS AND COMMUNITY WORK

I had always been interested in politics and when a ward vacancy came up, I applied and got the role. It had a hectic schedule of weekly meetings, responding to letters, visiting people and businesses in the city whilst running the stores. I gave it my all and made many great friends and connections in this time.

I also liked to get involved in community work whenever I could. So, at the same time I also chaired many committees, was elected school chairman of governors for Plymstock school and later Ridgeway school in Plympton, as well as being on the boards of several primary schools.

Photo: Award being presented at Plymstock School

I was very active as a Devon County Councillor at this time. I was part of the Domestic Coal Consumers Council.

Photo: Coal Consumers Council Meeting

I had a busy life with all of this and would say I didn't give the marriage or my wife the time they deserved and so we divorced. I gave up our house in Derriford to Valerie and decided it was time for a new start.

I hadn't quite found my way to complete happiness. A friend of mine, an ex-marine Jack Hunter, offered me to come and live with him till I sorted my life out. I remember saying I just wanted to have some quiet time, as I was at work all the time.

After some time, I was looking for my own property again and came across a house for sale in Yealmpton,

Devon. It was close enough to travel to Plymouth every day but felt like I was away from the store when at home. I bought it with a mortgage, it had an allotment and an orchard. I loved it and was quite happy there. The property had some stables on it which I converted into houses. I later also developed part of the orchard that wasn't working well into a swimming pool.

It was at this time I also wanted to start to look for property for my own store. In 1970, I opened a store on Embankment Road, in Plymouth. 'Larry Speare Carpet and Bed Furnishings,' consolidating some of the others I had run previously. Business was still doing well, and this settled my fears about rents and increasing bills.

Photo: Embankment Road Store

In 1972 I had the opportunity to purchase land which had just a little shed building with a tin roof and a cobbled floor. It was an old Anderson air raid shelter. I sold beds from here for a while. I was approached to buy land next door that had a garage and flats on it in Rendle Street, Plymouth. A lady asked me if I wanted to purchase it as her husband had died and she needed the money. I remember being happy to have it but made sure she was fairly compensated.

Then a lady from America called me up one day, I'd never met her in person, but she owned a warehouse next to the land and asked if I wanted to purchase this. I did. I changed the garage into a large parking space. I opened a carpet and bed store from the warehouse and it was a success again.

In 1980 I closed all the other stores and consolidated the shops into the one store on Rendle street.

Photo: Rendle Street Plot of Land

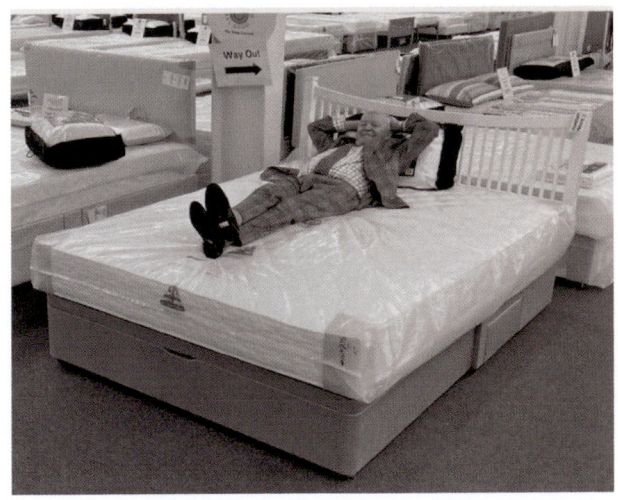

Photo: Larry in office in Rendle Street

Photo: Larry photo for advert

8 MEETING SHIRLEY AND BUILDING LARRY SPEARE

I used to drive to work every day along the same road from Yealmpton. I was single for six years and then one day I noticed a girl at the bus stop waiting to go to Plymouth. The next day she was there again and again: One day I decided to stop and ask her if she wanted a lift. I introduced myself and she said she knew who I was. We got chatting and she worked at Robert Daniels, Plymstock, Plymouth. This was how I met Shirley. I started giving her a lift to work each day.

Then we started seeing each other more regularly and I asked her out for drinks and to a concert. Her sister Jen came and we all got along. I met her parents, I'm not sure her mum approved though as she could see I was a lot older. However, we fell in love and got married at the United Reform Church in 1981.

Photo: Wedding Day Bridesmaids: LEFT TO RIGHT: Amanda, Kay, Sally, Elaine and Louise. Steve Endean with chimney sweep

Photo: Wedding Day BACK LEFT TO RIGHT: Shirley's Dad, Shirley's Mum, Karen, Shirley's Auntie and Uncle. NEXT TO BRIDE: David Bassett Best Man

In 1982 I commissioned the building you see today to be built in its place. Planning took a long time as these things do. I knew how I wanted it laid out. I had a very specific vision of a two storey large building that would hold a vast amount of stock and amaze people with choice when they came to see us.

Photo: Old Building on Rendle Street, before new one was built

During this process we found a very large air raid shelter. It is still under the current car park. We sealed the entrance so it would need to be dug up to access it, as I didn't want to disturb it with hundreds of people visiting. There was a lot of local and national interest in it. The entrance is by the garage roller door, and it is about the same size as the car park. So, you couldn't put a building in this area without changing or disturbing it. There are still a few odd items down there like some rusty metal bunks and buckets etc.

Photo: Hole in car park for access to shelter

Photo: Construction of new store

This one major store 'Larry Speare' on Rendle Street Plymouth has over 30,000 square feet of sales floor, a huge car park, and a massive warehouse. I worked 7 days a week to make the business a success. I always had worked hard; my mission was to own it myself and keep the business profitable.

Photo: Construction of New Store

Photo: New Store

To make it a success I had to get the name out there. I used the strength of advertising to do this. I put a lot of time into sharing the name through radio advertising. I contacted the local radio station, Plymouth Radio, and asked them if I could do my own adverts. They agreed and so I wrote and sang my own jingles, acting the fool but for which people would recognise and think of the business long after hearing the advert.

Photo: Larry in the recording studio late 2017

'My name is Larry Speare, I sell carpets and beds, there's no delay, you can have them today, my name is Larry Speare.' To be probably the most recalled.

The local radio station could see how well they were working and asked me to come in and do a regular slot not just with the adverts but speaking to callers who called in with questions. This is where the catchphrase 'EVERYONE KNOWS THAAAAAT' came from as I used to say it to callers after they asked a question. Again, acting the fool and becoming memorable, I knew this would help the business.

I interviewed celebrities once a week including Norman Wisdom, Alvin Stardust, Frankie Howard, Richard Murdoch, Helen Worth, Tony Sellby, Harry Corbett and Sooty and Sweep, to name just a few that we had great fun with.

Shirley and I used to host the celebrities that visited Plymouth offering them 'digs' in the houses I had converted from the stables.

Photo: Interview photo for newspaper

Alvin Stardust was so much fun, and Shirley loved making dinner for Frankie Howard when he was playing down at the Palace Theatre.

Photo: LEFT TO RIGHT: Shirley Speare, Larry Speare, and Alvin Stardust

Photo: LEFT TO RIGHT: Sooty, Harry Corbett, Sweep and Larry Speare

Photo: LEFT TO RIGHT: Richard Murdock, Helen Worth, Michel Angelis, Tony Selby and Larry Speare

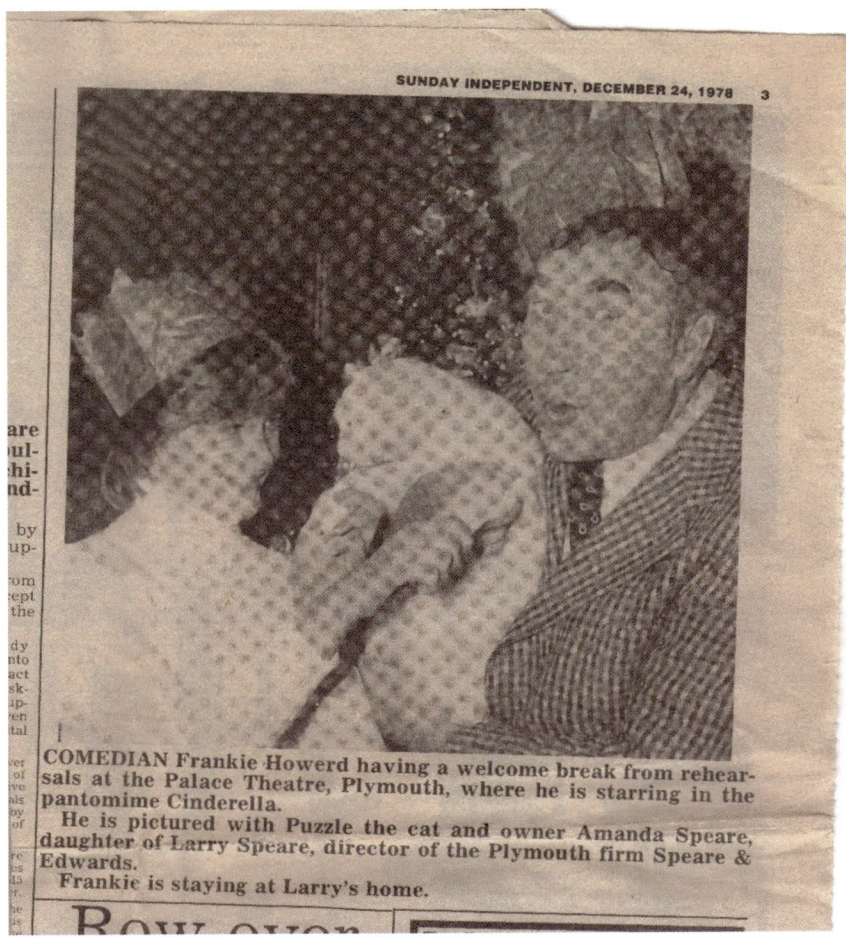

SUNDAY INDEPENDENT, DECEMBER 24, 1978   3

are
ul-
hi-
nd-

by
up-

om
ept
the

dy
nto
act
sk-
up-
en
tal

ver
of
ve
als
by
of

re
us
15
r.

be
at

COMEDIAN Frankie Howerd having a welcome break from rehearsals at the Palace Theatre, Plymouth, where he is starring in the pantomime Cinderella.

He is pictured with Puzzle the cat and owner Amanda Speare, daughter of Larry Speare, director of the Plymouth firm Speare & Edwards.

Frankie is staying at Larry's home.

Photo: LEFT TO RIGHT: Amanda Speare, Puzzle the Cat, and Frankie Howard

I then started advertising on local transport like the Torpoint Ferry and City Bus. I started off small but ended up having whole buses wrapped. It's funny because I still talk to people who remember them now.

Photo: CityBus wrapped 1980's

I tried to keep everything fresh, new and exciting. Changing shop layouts, having sales, advertising to keep the name remembered, offering same day delivery, and wowing the customers with great service and a fun experience when they came in. I have always worked and been present on the shop floor and would know exactly what was going on day to day.

Photo: CityBus wrapped 1970's

Photo: CityBus wrapped 2007

Photo: Larry on the shop floor

Shirley and I spent many years travelling directly to carpet manufacturers in Europe and here in the UK. France was a regular trip and Belgium. I had worked out that you could potentially cut out the wholesalers by buying direct, to not only save money but to get the best deals. I could then sell direct to customers at a cheaper rate, saving them money but at the same time increasing the profits.

The many manufacturers we went to became close contacts. We would often be put up in nice hotels, where we would socialise before getting to the wheeling and dealing the next day.

Photo: Shirley and Larry Speare on trip

I was invited to Atlanta America on a trip to meet a new manufacturer with other wholesalers from across the UK. It was an excellent trip. While I was there the city mayoress asked me to give a talk. She said I love hearing you talk 'limey' another nickname I had acquired!

Believe it or not I don't really like public speaking, but I did my best, and the talk went well. I just treat everyone the same no matter their background or level of education. I am determined and as my mother would say 'stubborn.' This stood me in good stead with the council work I was doing for the conservative party. I chaired the Road Safety Council and was often asked to join a committee or be a voice for others.

Photo: Larry Speare talking to American Audience

ET Barwick Industries, Inc.
World's largest maker of tufted carpets

B line News

Special Issue   (Printed in U.S.A.)   CHAMBLEE, GEORGIA   October, 1971

A group photo was made during the visit to Monsanto. Shown are (front row, from left) Larry Speare, Plymouth; Gordon Rowlands, Dursley; Bob Sayer, Cannock; Peter Dacey, Shepton Mallet; George Gipps, Sudbury, Suffolk; Les Whiston, Blackpool; Van Palmer, Birmingham; Steffan Larsen, Sandnes, Norway; Leif Jakobsen, Kristiansand, Norway. Second row: Ted Smale, Barwick-U.K.; John Hopkins, Swindon; Ted Hocknell Llandudno, North Wales; Pat Elms, Monsanto-London; Bob Williams, Barwick-U.K.; Tom Reid, Brighton; Ivan Skar, Oslo, Norway. Third row: Tony Clayton, Barwick-U.K.; Jim Healy, Barwick-U.K.; Cliff Heaven, Birmingham; Terry Kendall, Barwick-U.K.; Rolf Johansen, Sandefjord, Norway; Kaj Andersson, Malmo, Sweden; Tony Mitchell, Barwick-U.K. Fourth row: Michael Ford, London; Graham Thompson, Monsanto-London; Joy Lawrence, Carpet Review-London; Sven Larsen, Barwick-U.K.; John Glosby, Sudbury, Suffolk; Bryan Bownas, Barwick-U.K.; Charles Edwards, Plymouth. Back row: Barrie Bryant, Manchester; Frank McKelvey, Belfast; George Bryant, Manchester; George Abbott, London; Adrian Hyman, Belfast; Alan Ashworth, Barwick-U.K.; Douglas Froggatt, Hyde, Cheshire; Geoff Lewis, Gateshead; John Chicken, Barwick-U.K.; Larry Crenshaw, E. T. Barwick Industries; Gerald Ross, Glasgow; Ivar Ross, Glasgow; Stig Jonsson, Gothenburg, Sweden; Malcolm Dixie, Exeter. Not present for photo: Bernard Clyne, Barwick-U.K.; Peter Deano, Barwick-U.K., Crew; Neville Parish, Norwich; Lee Roper, E. T. Barwick Industries.

U. K. DEALERS INVADE GEORGIA

The Regency Hyatt House Hotel (left foreground) on Atlanta's famed Peachtree Street was headquarters for the group during their Georgia stay. Atop the hotel is a unique revolving restaurant, Polaris.

On an afternoon in late September Les Whiston, a Barwick carpet dealer from Blackpool, England, delivered personally a message from the mayor of Blackpool to the mayor of Atlanta.

While Mr. Whiston was in Mayor Sam Massell's office, many of his fellow dealers — customers of the Barwick plant in Bolton, England — were at Atlanta's East Lake Country Club playing golf with Sam Snead and Lee Trevino.

For the dealers, these were only two high points of what will be remembered as "the week that was."

They came from England, Scotland, Ireland, Wales, Norway and Sweden. Their "invasion" of Georgia began on Tuesday, Sept. 21, when they landed at Atlanta's Hartsfield International Airport.

During the seven days of their stay, the dealers participated in a number of activities that made for

what one dealer called "a once-in-a-lifetime experience."

Shortly after arriving at their hotel — the Regency Hyatt House on world-famous Peachtree Street — the group attended a reception hosted by E. T. Barwick, chairman of E. T. Barwick Industries, Inc., and other Barwick officials.

Other highlights of "the week that was":

Wednesday — The group was taken on a bus tour of Atlanta-area attractions, including Stone Mountain, the world's largest mass of exposed granite. They also visited a large carpet dealer.

Thursday — The group spent the day touring Barwick's manufacturing plants in Dalton and Lafayette, Georgia.

Friday — Monsanto Chemical Company took the group to Decatur, Alabama, for a tour of its fiber manufacturing plant.

(Continued on Page 2)

Photo: New Article October 1971. Larry bottom left front row.

Special Edition   October, 1971

B-LINE NEWS

2

U. K. DEALERS INVADE GEORGIA

The Barwick B-Line News is the exclusive publication of the employes of E. T. Barwick Industries, Inc., and its subsidiaries.

(Continued from Page 1)

Saturday — The dealers visited Barwick's international headquarters at Chamblee, Georgia, a suburb of Atlanta.

Monday — A golf outing with U. S. Open champion Lee Trevino and veteran pro Sam Snead, followed by an old fashioned Southern cookout-style dinner.

Tuesday — A tour of the Atlanta Merchandise Mart, the home of frequent home furnishings merchandise shows.

Accompanying the dealers were key sales executives of Barwick

United Kingdom, including Alan Ashworth, sales manager for the Bolton plant.

Also in the group were two representatives of Monsanto Chemical Co. and a writer for "Carpet Review," a British trade publication.

"It was a fruitful week for all of us," said Lee Roper, Barwick's vice president for foreign operations.

"It gave us a chance to show our appreciation to these dealers for the fine job they are doing in selling Barwick carpets in their areas. It also enabled them to get to know

our company better by visiting our international headquarters at Chamblee and our plants at Dalton and Lafayette.

"Without dealers like these, our company could not have achieved the worldwide success it has enjoyed in recent years."

Sales abroad are a growing part of Barwick's business. In its latest annual report, the company said that sales of foreign operations rose 25 per cent— to $16,787,622— in fiscal 1971. The company's total sales for the period were $158,123,256.

Photo: UK Dealers visiting America – Larry third from right standing

59

Public life was not always easy. It certainly came with its challenges. I spent six years defending my name in one libel case.

Photo: Herald newspaper June 1985

In hindsight I can say the publicity eventually helped! But it was a tough time to go through.

Jubilant . . Larry Speare after his victory.

admitted he missed the hurly-burly of life as a councillor. "My weakness is politics," he said. "I love the cut and thrust of it. I love the arguments and the achievements, even if you do have to take a lot of knocks.

"I'm a man of action and I suppose it calls for the sort of drive I put into my business affairs. I always felt I had to get involved in local goings-on; it wasn't any use standing on the outside. I had to join and do something."

At the height of the Plympton St. Mary ward row, he finally defended his seat there as an Independent at the 1979 City Council elections. "I had no option," he said. "It was the only way I could get a platform."

But he lost, and promptly resigned the seat he held on Devon County Council.

He does not rule out a return to council benches, though. "If I had won my seat six years ago, I would have immediately applied for the Conservative Whip," he said.

"I am still a member of the Party — I belong to the Plymstock Radford branch — and I could make a come-back. Anything is possible in this world."

He called on Mrs. Peggy Radmore to resign her seat forthwith. "She is a woman who has lost all credibility," he declared.

But Mrs. Radmore said she had no intention of resigning — and she planned to defend her seat

Photo: Herald newspaper June 1985

9 CHILDREN, FOOBALL AND PROUD ACHIEVEMENTS

Shirley and I went on to have 3 Children Taffeta in 1982, Kenny in 1983 and Henry 1991.

Photo: Plymstock School

I was still Chair of Governors when my own children went to Plymstock School.

Photo: Larry when governor at Plymstock School

I sponsored the school football team, both my sons played in the school and various other teams. We are a football-loving family.

Photo: Football Team with Larry Speare sponsor shirts

I decided to get involved with the Devon Wednesday League, 'Speare and Edwards' had a team in the early 1970's which was long before my boys were born.

Plymstock repeat city triumph after second half blitz

PLYMSTOCK under-15 boys' football team beat Devonport High School for Boys 6-1 to retain their Plymouth Schools' title.

In a hard-fought first-half, Plymstock opened the scoring with a great shot from Joe Jasper, who went on to score a hat-trick. Another goal from S Jude made it 2-0.

However, from a set-piece DHS reduced the gap to 2-1 before half-time, but the second period belonged to Plymstock.

Substitute J Hocken opened the scoring after the break and then the goals started to come from all angles, with three more following.

Mark Taylor, Plymstock's head of PE, said: "This was a great game of football between two even sides.

"I am incredibly proud of the boys, who have been committed and dedicated to training over the past four years.

"I know the boys were disappointed to not reach the county finals after being knocked out in the semi-finals two years running.

"But to win the Plymouth title is testament to their perseverance.

"I must also thank all the parents for their continued support towards the team and our sponsor Larry Speare."

Meanwhile, the school have also been crowned Plymouth champions at Panathlon. Their success will see them represent the city at the national finals in Liverpool next month.

The Panathlon is a multi-discipline event which involves activities ranging from athletics, chess, cycling, orienteering, boys and girls football, basketball, netball, badminton, and table tennis.

The event was hosted by Marjons and involved more than 300 pupils from Plymstock, Lipson, Coombe Dean and DHS. Plymstock prevailed and go through to compete against schools from London, Bristol, Leeds and Liverpool for the national title. All pupils received medals for their participation.

Taylor added: "This is a great event which involves many pupils from all year groups.

"In a sense this is a full school event.

"Not only does it involve sporting ability, but also intelligence such as the chess and orienteering events.

"It is great to see many pupils competing and reinforces what a fantastic event this is in bringing pupils together.

"At Plymstock School, we strongly believe in participation and this event really reinforces

Photo: Football Team, proud of how hard they worked

I cannot really remember how it all came about becoming the official sponsor, or when, but I loved it! I used to attend as many games as I could and sponsor individual teams. I met so many amazing people over the years and I kept as many newspaper clippings as I could of all the games and presentations.

PHOTO: Herald newspaper

Devon Wednesday league winners - Larry Speare captain Lee Dare City College Plymouth

It has been fun looking over them and remembering all the good times when putting this book together.

Photo: Herald newspaper Devon Wednesday league referee award – Respect for Referees

Photo: Herald newspaper Devon Wednesday league winners

Photo: Herald newspaper Devon Wednesday league winners - Lipson Community College FROM LEFT: Corey Tippett, Jack Neal, Jack Newham, Kris Kearney, Larry Speare, Craig Swiggs and Steve Lyndon

Photo: Herald newspaper Devon Wednesday League Winners- City Police FROM LEFT: Mike Richards, Graham Kirkup, Larry Speare and Ken Ord

Photo: Football Team with Larry Speare sponsor shirts – Marine Academy Juniors

I also got involved with the Argyle youth development team and talent spotters. I regularly gave donations for kit. I loved being able to help the kids.

Photo: Argyle Youth development sponsorship

Photo: Argyle Youth development sponsorship

It was great publicity but that's not why I did it, I liked helping and being part of it all. I liked seeing the boys develop their skills and was lucky enough to attend some cracking games.

Talent spotters keep try thanks to Larry

PLYMOUTH Argyle Youth Development's talent spotters have had all-weather coats bought for them after a £500 donation from city businessman Larry Speare.

Argyle have 20-plus scouts who are all out and about, whatever the weather, checking out young players.

Youth development officer John James said he was very grateful for the continued support of Larry Speare.

"Larry has been our longest and most consistent donor and benefactor over the years, looking for no reward except for a share in the success of the boys who go through and make it to the professional level," said James.

"A lot of boys have him to thank for what he has done for them behind the scenes over the years and he should not be forgotten.

"The Youth Development is self-supporting and is extremely grateful for any help we get so a big 'thank you' to Larry.

"If any of our supporters would like to follow in Larry's shoes, please contact me at Home Park on Plymouth 562561."

SUPPORT PLAY: Larry Speare (second right) presents Argyle youth development officer John James (second left) with the new all-weather coats

Photo: Argyle talent spotters Larry Speare Sponsored uniform

I am a big believer in Argyle, they have helped the community of Plymouth massively over the years and if I could be a part of that I too wanted to help. I went to watch many matches, those of the youth teams and coaching sessions as well.

PLYMOUTH Argyle have had no delay in finding a new sponsor for their centre of excellence teams.

■ by SARA RAINE

Local businessman Larry Speare has agreed to sponsor the club's under-12s, under-13s, under-14s and under-15 sides.

It is the first time anyone has agreed to sponsor all the teams, which has delighted the club.

"It's splendid and we're extremely grateful," said Argyle chief executive David Tall.

"These teams are a very important building block in the construction of Plymouth Argyle."

Although neither party wanted to reveal how much the sponsorship was worth, Argyle associate director Ken Jones said: "It's a very, very generous sponsorship deal."

Jones added: "Over the years PAYD has been running the youth set up and sponsorship has been vital.

"In the past it has been difficult, but things are looking up now.

"Larry has come up and offered to sponsor four teams, and so he becomes the outright sponsor of the youth set up.

"It's the first time we've had one major sponsor.

"It's a one year deal, but we hope Larry may come along next year and continue.

"His name will appear on the shirts of the teams, on all the tracksuits, on advertising around the ground and in the programme."

Speare has a keen interest in junior football and has seen at

first hand the work that goes on at the club's centre of excellence, which attract youngsters from all over Devon, Cornwall and even Somerset.

He said he was only too happy to help the club continue their work with young footballers in the West Country.

"It does give me great pleasure to contribute," said Speare.

"I've been involved with football for many, many years.

"I sponsor the Devon Wednesday League cups.

"And I feel very strongly about what Argyle have done in recent years, providing this service to the community, making sure kids are doing something useful.

Gratitude

"You just have to look at the coaching that goes on twice a week at Ivybridge.

"I've been around many different centres of excellence and I can sincerely say that, in my opinion, Argyle can more than match any other clubs for coaching – it's superb.

"So I thought I would do something to show my gratitude."

Speare, who said he lives for football, added: "Kids receive a lot of top-class coaching, which helps improve local football as well."

Speare is likely to be seen watching the centre of excellence teams.

He added: "I'm doing this for my love of football and it's where the future is."

SPEARE WE GO: Larry Speare (left) meets Argyle associate director Ken Jones after being named centre of excellence sponsor

Photo: Argyle Youth development sponsorship

In 1983 Shirley and I moved and purchased another house in Yealmpton. A house we have now lived in for over 40 years.

In September 2009, a day I never forget happened. A man stabbed my wife Shirley, in an unprovoked attack, whilst walking our dog Archie in the village where we had always lived. She had to spend nearly three weeks in hospital because her lung was punctured. I was so worried. We all were. The person was caught and found guilty of attempted murder.

Photo: Herald Article

In 2015 I celebrated 50 years in business and won a lifetime achievement award from the Plymouth Herald. This was a great honour and a very emotional night.

Photo: Herald Article

PAGE 2   The Herald, Wednesday April 29 2015

Herald Business Awards

Honouring those driving

by WILLIAM TELFORD
Business editor ✪ @WTelfordHerald

THERE was glitz, glamour, music, laughter and even a few tears when the leading lights of Plymouth's business community celebrated the success of entrepreneurs, companies – and the city itself.

The Herald Business Awards reflected a year of achievement by Plymouth's premier business names, with 16 winners taking home prizes.

And it was generally acknowledged that the black-tie extravaganza, which attracted more than 500 people to Plymouth Pavilions, was a huge success in its own right.

With special guest England rugby star Phil Vickery providing the laughs, with a witty and enjoyable speech, and EastEnders actress Hetti Bywater, the co-host, adding a touch of razzle-dazzle to an already glamorous occasion, it was down to carpet and bed magnate Larry Speare to draw a tear, with a touching tribute to his wife Shirley as he accepted the Lifetime Achievement Award.

The Businesses of the Year were named as the Princess Yachts International, Carval Computing, and Alpha Logic.

Other prominent winners, all of whom received a specially framed "front page" shout their firm's success, included Column Bakehouse, Dura Manufacturing, Sponge UK, Santander Plymouth, Devonport Guildhall, Fairfield Electronics, Plymouth City Council, the Treby Arms, and Kawasaki Precision Engineering.

David Rowe, boss of Applied Automation, was named Entrepreneur of the Year, while Clare McCombe, of equine care business Flint's Yard, was the Young Business Person of the Year.

Mark Sainsbury, managing director of The Herald's parent firm DC Media, opened what he described as one of the city's "most anticipated events" by praising the quality of all the businesses nominated – and, indeed, that entered.

"You are all winners in our eyes," he said.

And he outlined how prosperous the city has become and said: "This year the economic landscape has changed and many businesses across Plymouth are feeling buoyant with confidence on the up.

"Companies are starting to invest in their premises and employees and new businesses are coming to Plymouth."

He said that included The Herald's parent firm DC Media, which is investing in new products and developing new platforms and recently added 13 staff to its 280-strong workforce.

Paul Burton, editor of The Herald, co-hosting the awards alongside Miss Bywater, said the shortlisted nominees, and winners, had been whittled down from an astonishing 450 entries.

He stressed: "We noticed the quality of entries had changed, with some that had previously been in the Small Business category were now Medium-sized, an encouraging sign."

And he said the number of entries received from Plymouth Science Park-based firms had been "exceptional".

It meant, he said, Plymouth was now starting to reach its full potential.

"Plymouth is a hotbed of entrepreneurial talent," he said. "It's a place people want to do business in."

Nick Holman, chairman of governors at City College Plymouth, the headline sponsor, also gave a speech.

He told the assembled businesses how the college, celebrating its 125th anniversary, played a central role in the economic life of the city.

Highlighting the college's plan for an exiting £13million STEM (science, technology, engineering and maths) centre, he stressed it will "continue to deliver high-quality learning opportunities" for the city, identifying future training needs and tackling any skills gap.

The awards were presented by representatives from the firms and organisations sponsoring the categories.

The list included: Jane Jones from First Great Western; Fergus Scarfe from GOD TV; Tracey Lawes from Aqua Training; Christian Jenkins from Plymouth Science Park; Alison Fine from Outset Plymouth; Ross Mackenzie from Courier Force; Lisa Davey from HD Diagnostics; Adam Spiers from jeweller Michael Spiers; Mark Russell of Optimus Performance Marketing; Natalie Wooldridge from MGB; Lesley Bunce from Slice A Pizza; Peter Hartland from Plymouth Chamber of Commerce; Nikolaos Tzokas from Plymouth University; and Phil Davies and Sharron Robbie of City College Plymouth.

Other sponsors included Le Vignoble, S&H Technical Support, which was also responsible for the decor in the Pavilions arena, and Drakes Group, which provided raffle prizes.

Music was provided by Plymouth Symphony Orchestra.

A raffle raised £2,950 for the event's charity, Macmillan Cancer Support.

NIGHT OFF: The Herald's Business Editor William Telford

Laughter, tears and love for our Larry

THERE was an emotional moment when bed and carpet king Larry Speare was announced as the recipient of this year's Herald Lifetime Achievement Award.

The mogul, one of the most instantly recognisable figures in Plymouth's business community, received a standing ovation as he made it way to the Pavilions stage to accept the honour.

Mr Speare was cheered and applauded and reacted by wiping away a tear as he took to the mic to thank his staff, his family, his friends, and The Herald.

And, with typical good humour, he said: "For those that don't know me my name is Larry Speare."

Then he added: "I sell carpets and beds. There's no delay, you can have them today."

Mr Speare is, of course, the boss and founder of one of Plymouth's most distinctive businesses, the Stonehouse-based Larry Speare Ltd bed and carpet company.

He joked that the publicity he will receive from winning the award will cover the ticket price and booze bill for attending the awards night.

He then listed those he wanted to thank, including Plymouth and Devon Chamber of Commerce, his friend David Whitfield, from the Hoe's Squires Guest House, and his workforce.

"No one could do this without good quality staff behind them," he said.

He also highlighted the contribution of his family, including his sons David, Kenny and Henry.

"They're in the business and as I fade away they will take over and become the future," he said.

But he saved the most important "thank you" until last – it was for his wife Shirley.

"I love you darling," he said, bringing the house down.

"We built the business together and she is everything to me," he said. "She's the most important person in my life. We married 35 years ago and have three fabulous kids and a beautiful granddaughter."

Mr Speare was honoured in a competitive category for his lifetime in business.

He has been an entrepreneur since childhood, when as one of six children brought up in a tiny cottage, he would get up early to pick mushrooms and berries to sell to shops.

At 15, he became an apprentice at a furniture shop, rising to assistant manager, turned around the fortunes of another carpet firm, and decided to go into business for himself.

He sold his only asset – a Ford Anglia – to take out a lease on a shop in Cornwall Street in 1985.

After a year, he opened a second shop, and the business grew and relocated.

He bought an old garage with a tin

Photo: Herald Article

I've always prided myself on being selective with the shop staff we have, making sure they offer the highest level of service. We currently average a team of around fifteen.

I also have access to a team of highly qualified and experienced fitters, for quick, professional, and quality work, which has always served me and my customers well.

Many of my staff have worked with me for many years. Andrew, who works in our warehouse measuring and cutting flooring does so to the highest standard. He started to work for me when he left school at sixteen and is still with us today over 40 years on. A strange coincidence is his father was based in Malaya in the Marines at the same time as me, although we didn't know each other.

2018 and 2019 was when BREXIT was on everyone's minds but especially if you were in business. I thought it may be a 'choppy' ride but was willing to take the hit. I believed in BREXIT; I think decision making should be made here in the UK. At this point 90% of my stock was coming from Europe so I wasn't sure it was going to be good for the business. But I remember a time when we were not in the European Market and I didn't worry then. I knew I could get supply from countries outside of Europe if there were problems. As it happened and as

I expected it didn't affect the business too much at all.

Larry's prepared to take Brexit hit

'I KNOW WHERE TO BUY OUTSIDE EUROPE'

By MILES O'LEARY
miles.oleary@reachplc.com
@ph_milesoleary

PLYMOUTH business veteran Larry Speare admits his iconic brand may endure a choppy ride post-Brexit – but he's willing to take the hit in the name of national pride.

The legendary entrepreneur says the bulk of carpets sold from his home furnishings HQ come directly from sources in Europe he's built solid relationships with.

And the 86-year-old chief admits he's having to prepare for disruption by sending staff to seminars to brief them on tariffs which may be imposed at the border in the event of No Deal.

He may have to draw more heavily upon international clients in places like Turkey, India, Egypt and China if there's reams of red-tape to get through – which could increase costs.

But Larry's all in for Brexit because it'll take decision-making – and finances – away from the European political elite, he says.

Speaking exclusively to The Herald about Brexit and the potential repercussions, sharp-minded Larry said: "I don't think Brexit is particularly good for this business, because 90% of my large carpet turnover comes from Europe.

"When I started in business, it was all British made. But they managed to lose their way and the Europeans moved in, and produced a product that was suitable for most people's budgets.

"I have a very good relationship with the suppliers in Europe. And I go over there, two to three times a year, with my manager, my son, and we buy from source.

"We don't buy through wholesale. We cut out the middle man.

"We have very good friends over there – no question about it."

Larry, who set up shop in Rendle Street in 1980 and developed a cult following with his voice still regularly heard over the airwaves, says an agreed trade deal with Brussels is the way he'd prefer things to go.

"I do worry to a certain extent how this is going to go," he admitted. "If we get a result, a deal, it's going to be more advantageous for me, not only for me but lots and lots of businesses that import from Europe. The amount of red-tape coming out; I have staff going to seminars for a while, they are going to plan if this comes in or that comes in."

But Larry admits he's a 'little bit anti-European' by nature.

"Why should we give £350million (a week) to Europe, when that money can go to many worthy causes?" Larry said.

"That's what really gets under my skin. I know we have to pay an EU membership. But I have been in business for 55 years, and I can remember a time when there was no Brexit, no common market. And we excelled. Did I worry then? No, I didn't. I loved our independence."

Larry reckons he 'can handle' any short-term knock to his company – which he built up from scratch into a nationally-recognised carpets and beds empire despite local planners way back in the day telling him it'd never work.

"Sales will only be affected if you can't get sales," he said.

"I know where to get sales and it doesn't have to be from Europe.

"There are a lot of Chinese carpets sold in this country. We sell a lot of Indian, Egyptian and a lot of Middle Eastern countries make great fabrics as well. Carpets from these places have been coming over since before Brexit."

As for Boris? He's confident 'he can pull Brexit out of the fire.'

"I think that he is great, in that he is a very, very intelligent man, no question about it," Larry said.

"But lots of members of Parliament, they may be rich but they have never really grafted. They have never really experienced a day's work.

"They come out of posh college, and go into politics. They don't understand what is going on outside."

Photo: Herald Article

In 2019/2020 Covid came and just like everyone else we found ourselves confined to home. It was the longest I have ever been away from the business and the longest I had shut in over 50 years! We kept busy at home, going for walks and tending to the garden. I was worried about the business, well certainly the building, I didn't want it getting broken into or vandalised. When restrictions eased, I used the time to revamp the shop. We tidied, decorated and deep cleaned throughout to make sure we were ready for opening.

When we had heard the rumors of lockdowns, I wanted to be prepared so I contacted all the suppliers we had and bought a massive amount of stock. I spent a few 'bob' for sure. We took all our normal stock, which is plentiful anyway. I think it was the most stock we have ever held! This meant that when we reopened, we were not immediately affected by manufacturer shortages. People thought I was crazy doing this at this time but I have been called that many times in my life.

David, my son from my first marriage, joined the business. He was a successful carpet and vinyl rep and worked for the business until he retired in 2021. My sons Kenny and Henry joined the business when they left school and now run the departments day to day for me. Kenny runs the carpet department and Henry the bed department. They have improved the stock and selection, which has also improved the business. My wife Shirley has worked alongside me for as long as we have been together. She loves coming in and working alongside the family and the team.

Photo: LEFT TO RIGHT: Kenny Speare, Shirley Speare, Larry Speare, and Henry Speare

In 2022 I launched an online website shop for the first time ever. I don't get involved in this or social media, but I'm told by the younger team now this is an important part of the company's future.

God has been good to me, 58 years in business and 90 years of life, the business is still going strong, I still come in every week, and you may occasionally spot me on the shop floor. I don't think it's in my blood to retire. I am confident of the continued success of the business and I am immensely proud at how hard they all work. I hope one day my grandchildren may follow in my footsteps.

Photo: LEFT TO RIGHT: Kenny Speare, Taffeta Speare, Shirley Speare, Henry Speare and Larry Speare. The Ship Inn Noss Mayo for Henry's 21st Birthday

10 THANK YOU

And so that brings me to a conclusion for this book. I would like to thank all the people in my life not just those named but also many of the unnamed supporters, business connections, customers, staff, and friends I have made along the way. Whilst I am sure there are many more memories I could have shared and many stories surely forgotten, I hope this gives you a glimpse into the life and making of 'Larry Speare.'

ABOUT THE AUTHOR

Larry Speare has become one of the most instantly recognisable figures in Plymouth's business community. He founded the Plymouth based business Larry Speare Ltd. A bed and carpet company that is well known in Devon and Cornwall.

When he won The Herald's Lifetime Achievement honour in 2015, he joked: "For those that don't know me, my name is Larry Speare." Then he added: "I sell carpets and beds. There is no delay, you can have them today." Referring to his famous jingles and radio adverts.

Larry has been an entrepreneur since childhood. Born into poverty, one of six children and brought up in a tiny cottage in Plymouth, during the second world war, he was later conscripted to the Royal Marines before leaving and becoming an apprentice at a furniture shop, rising to assistant manager before deciding to go into business for himself.

He has been in business 56 years and at age 90 he thought it was about time to record some of his interesting life events and stories, into a book, so that you can learn a bit more about his life and the person behind the iconic name 'Larry Speare'.

To date Larry Speare still comes into the shop a couple of times a week!

Printed in Great Britain
by Amazon